9-

P9-DMA-192

Happy 6th B-Day
Connor

Love, Grandma
+ Papa

# EMMET TO THE RESCUE

by Julia March

**Senior Editor** Tori Kosara
**Senior Designer** Anna Formanek
**Designer** Sam Bartlett
**Design Assistant** James McKeag
**US Proofreader** Megan Douglass
**Pre-production Producer** Marc Staples
**Producer** Louise Daly
**Managing Editor** Paula Regan
**Managing Art Editor** Jo Connor
**Publisher** Julie Ferris
**Art Director** Lisa Lanzarini
**Publishing Director** Simon Beecroft

Dorling Kindersley would like to thank Randi Sørensen,
Heidi K. Jensen, Paul Hansford, and Martin Leighton Lindhardt
at the LEGO Group.

First American Edition, 2019
Published in the United States by DK Publishing
345 Hudson Street, New York, New York 10014

19 20 21 22 23  10 9 8 7 6 5 4 3 2 1
001–312560–Jan/2019

DK books are available at special discounts when
purchased in bulk for sales promotions, premiums,
fund-raising, or educational use. For details, contact:
DK Publishing Special Markets,
345 Hudson Street, New York, New York 10014
SpecialSales@dk.com

ISBN 978-1-4654-8038-5 (Hardcover)
ISBN 978-1-4654-7976-1 (Paperback)

Printed and bound in China

**www.dk.com**
**www.LEGO.com**

A WORLD OF IDEAS:
**SEE ALL THERE IS TO KNOW**

# Contents

# Emmet

Emmet is a cheerful guy.
He rides a special bike.
Emmet lives in a city.

# Aliens attack

Emmet has five good friends.
They are Lucy, Unikitty, Benny,
Metalbeard, and Batman.
Oh no!
Aliens come from space.
They attack the city.

Benny

Metalbeard

Lucy

Unikitty

Batman

# Sweet Mayhem

Sweet Mayhem is a space pilot.
She kidnaps Emmet's friends.
They fly away in her spaceship.

# Space rescue

Emmet wants to rescue
his friends.
He builds his own spaceship.
Then he flies into space to
look for them.

Emmet's friends

# Rex

Rex is a space pilot.
He sees that Emmet
is in danger.
Will Rex save Emmet?

**Emmet and Rex**

# Rex's spaceship

Rex has a spaceship.
It looks like a big fist.
The ship has a crew
of dinosaurs.

# The crew

The dinosaurs help Rex
on his spaceship.
They are always busy.

The dinosaurs are
ready for danger.
This one has two
laser cannons.

The dinosaurs
take breaks.
They drink coffee.

This dinosaur has wings.
He can fly.

The dinosaurs love
to skateboard.
It is fun!

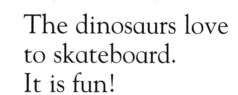

# New friends

Rex saves Emmet from danger.
Emmet likes Rex.

# Teamwork

Emmet looks for his friends with Rex.

They are ready for an
adventure!

# Quiz

1. Where does Emmet live?

2. Who kidnaps Emmet's friends?

3. Who does Emmet want to find?

4. What do the dinosaurs love to do?

5. Who saves Emmet from danger?

# Index

**Answers to the quiz on page 22**
1. In a city 2. Sweet Mayhem 3. His friends
4. Skateboard 5. Rex

# A LEVEL FOR EVERY READER

This book is a part of an exciting four-level reading series to support children in developing the habit of reading widely for both pleasure and information. Each book is designed to develop a child's reading skills, fluency, grammar awareness, and comprehension in order to build confidence and enjoyment when reading.

## Ready for a Level 1 (Learning to Read) book

A child should:
- be familiar with most letters and sounds.
- understand how to blend sounds together to make words.
- have an awareness of syllables and rhyming sounds.

## A valuable and shared reading experience

For many children, learning to read requires much effort, but adult participation can make reading both fun and easier. Here are a few tips on how to use this book with an early reader:

*Check out the contents together:*
- tell the child the book title and talk about what the book might be about.
- read about the book on the back cover and talk about the contents page to help heighten interest and expectation.
- chat about the pictures on each page.
- discuss new or difficult words.

*Support the reader:*
- give the book to the young reader to turn the pages.
- if the book seems too hard, support the child by sharing the reading task.

*Talk at the end of each page:*
- ask questions about the text and the meaning of the words used—this helps develop comprehension skills.
- read the quiz at the end of the book and encourage the reader to answer the questions, if necessary, by turning back to the relevant pages to find the answers.